Go Forth

REDEEMER
CITY to CITY

GLOBAL
FAITH & WORK
INITIATIVE
A MINISTRY OF REDEEMER CITY TO CITY

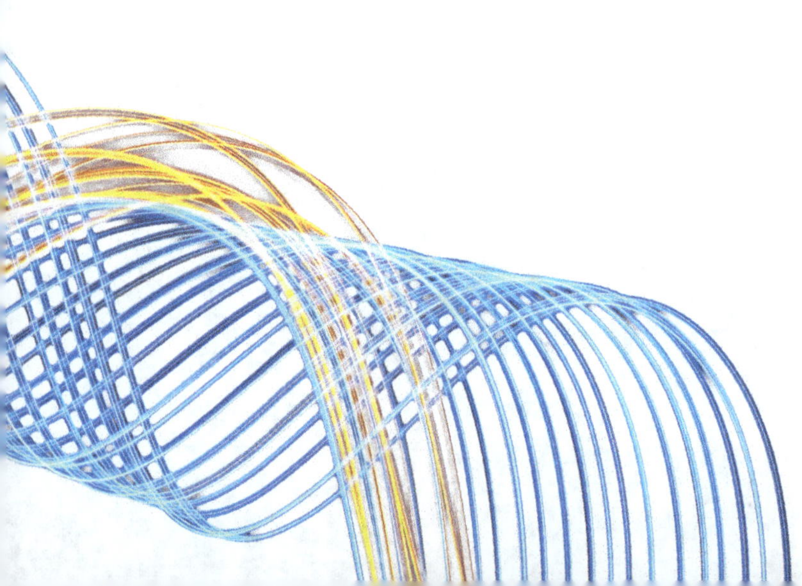

Go Forth

God's Purpose for Your Work

AN EIGHT-WEEK BIBLE STUDY
BY REDEEMER CITY TO CITY

Redeemer City to City
57 W. 57th Street
4th Floor
New York
NY 10019
United States

www.redeemercitytocity.com

ISBN 979-8-218-39087-7 (print)
ISBN 979-8-218-39391-5 (ebook)

Author: *Charlie Meo*
General Editor: *Lauren Gill*
Cover design and interior design: *Revo Creative*

And whatever you do, in word or deed,
do everything in the name of the Lord
Jesus, giving thanks to God the Father
through him.

COLOSSIANS 3:17

Contents

Introduction

What if we missed it?

For many Christians, the work we do every day is a means to a more "spiritual" end. We endure challenging meetings, countless spreadsheets, terrible commutes, and sometimes painful labor so that we can get to the *real* work God has called us to. We view work as an obstacle to our discipleship journey.

But what if it wasn't?

What if work was not an obstacle but part of God's perfect design? What if it was a pathway for your heart, your neighbor, and your city to experience renewal?

The math is simple. For every hour we spend in a church gathering, many of us will spend at least forty somewhere else—at work. It's time for us to consider how God might not only want to shape us on Sundays but also throughout our working week. God doesn't dismiss our everyday work but rather sees paid and unpaid work as vital to his redemptive mission. When Jesus returns, our work won't disappear. Rather, it will be perfectly redeemed and finally delivered from sin's tyranny.

This Bible study is an invitation to reimagine every vocation and workplace as an arena where God's character is on display. Through this guide, you will explore with others the beauty and brokenness of work—from the first lines of Scripture until the very last page.

But thinking about work differently isn't enough. We need new practices that transform our current work habits. And more than all of this, as Christians, we need the Holy Spirit to fill us anew for the work ahead.

Let's not miss it. Let's begin to see work as a crucial on-ramp to experience the power of the gospel in our work lives.

How to Use This Bible Study

Whether you're the group leader or simply a participant, below are some guidelines on how to get the best out of this Bible study. For each of the eight weeks, you will be given an introduction, a time to prepare yourself to hear what God is saying through his Word, scriptural passages to focus on, discussion questions, a practice for the following week, and a commissioning prayer. At the end of each week, there are also some notes for the group leader to help lead the session. Below is a brief outline of each of the course components.

1 Introduction

Each session begins by introducing the theme and core insights for that week. The goal is to provide a framework for where you will be journeying.

2 Ready

It's easy to jump into reading Scripture without taking a moment to prepare yourself to listen to God. Every time you pick up the Bible, an encounter with God is possible. Each week, ready yourself to enter God's presence and hear his voice by saying a prayer together, followed by two minutes of quiet reflection.

3 Read

Reading the Bible out loud is a powerful practice. After the group has sat in silence for two minutes, choose one person in the group to read the Bible passage/s. Then choose a different person to read through the passage/s again. After each Bible passage, there is a "Key References" section, which unpacks significant concepts for that week.

4 Reflect

The goal of this section is for the group to dialogue together about what insights and questions come to mind as you hear God's Word. There are discussion questions to guide the conversation. At the end of each week, there are also additional notes to help the leader guide the discussion.

5 Respond

The goal of this Bible study is not to create anxious activity but *prayerful response* to what God is revealing to each person. Each week, there will be a practical way for you to respond to what you are learning that is directly related to your work.

6 Release

View the end of each study as a release into God's world for the good work he has called you to. Each week there is a commissioning prayer for you to stand and recite together.

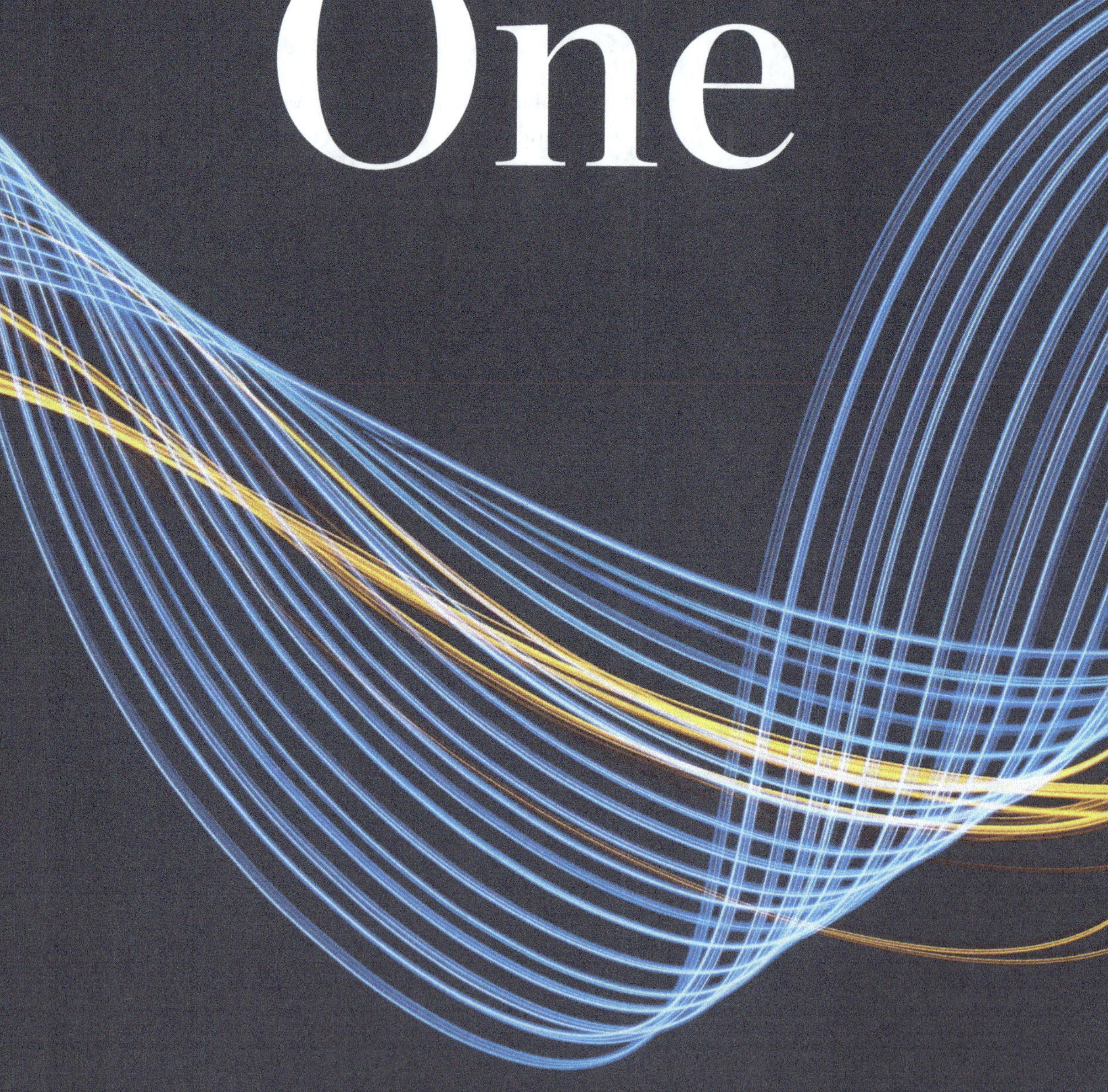

Week
One

Made to Work

(GENESIS 1–2)

Introduction

We are about to begin an eight-week journey exploring how work is not a nuisance to the Christian witness but *integral* to the mission of seeing the kingdom of God come on earth as it is in heaven. Regardless of this fact, many of us may only see the brokenness, sin, and deformation that happens in and through our work. The goal of Week One is to renew our vision of work from being a byproduct of the fall to part of the good creation of God. The story of work does not begin with the sin in Genesis 3; it begins in Genesis 1 with truth, goodness, and beauty. Let's explore this incredible reality together.

Ready

The unbelievable truth is this: You are about to hear God speak. Every time you pick up the Bible, an encounter with God is possible. First, ready yourself to enter God's presence and hear his voice. To begin, offer this simple prayer to God and then wait in silence for two minutes:

Father, help me hear your voice.
Jesus, help me sense your presence.
Spirit, help me live according to your ways.

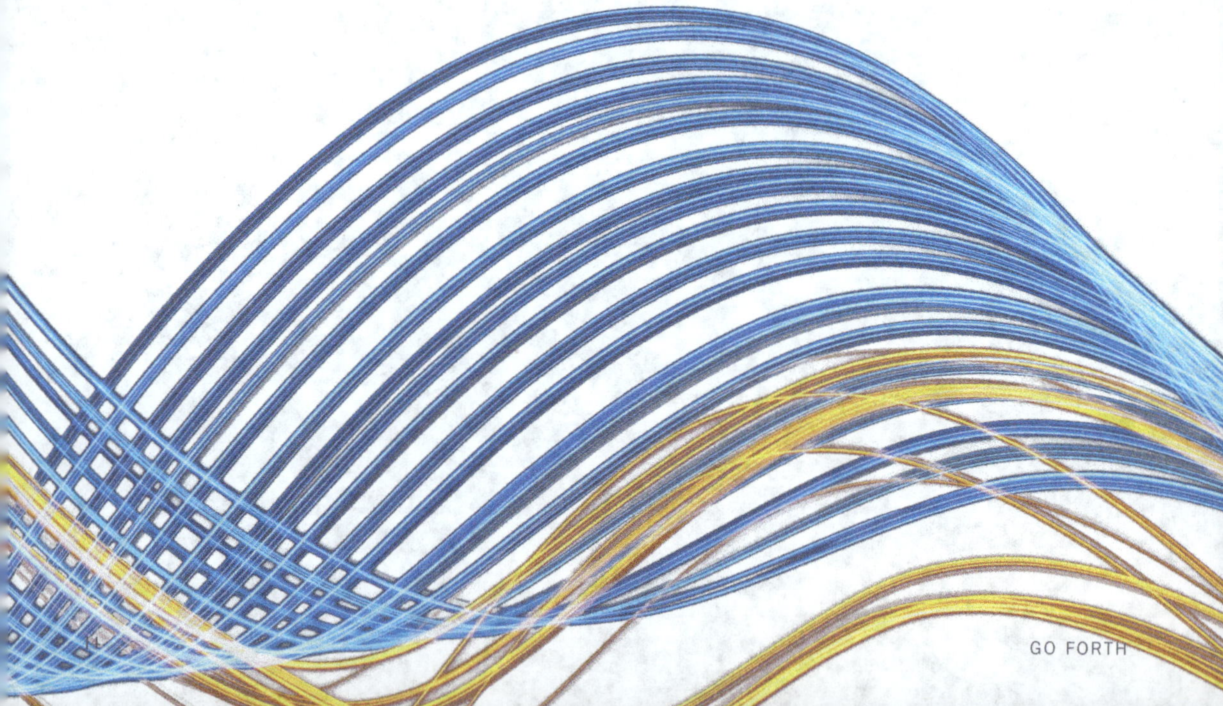

Read

After sitting in silence for two minutes, choose someone to read the passages below. Then choose a different person to read through the passages again.

Genesis 1:26–31:

26 Then God said, "Let us make man in our **image**, after our **likeness**. And let them have **dominion** over the fish of the sea and over the birds of the heavens and over the livestock and over all the earth and over every creeping thing that creeps on the earth."

27 So God created man in his own image, in the image of God he created him; male and female he created them.

28 And God blessed them. And God said to them, "Be fruitful and multiply and fill the earth and subdue it, and have **dominion** over the fish of the sea and over the birds of the heavens and over every living thing that moves on the earth." 29 And God said, "Behold, I have given you every plant yielding seed that is on the face of all the earth, and every tree with seed in its fruit. You shall have them for food. 30 And to every beast of the earth and to every bird of the heavens and to everything that creeps on the earth, everything that has the breath of life, I have given every green plant for food." And it was so. 31 And God saw everything that he had made, and behold, it was very good. And there was evening and there was morning, the sixth day.

Genesis 2:15–17:

15 The Lord God took the man and put him in the garden of Eden to work it and keep it. 16 And the Lord God commanded the man, saying, "You may surely eat of every tree of the garden, 17 but of the tree of the knowledge of good and evil you shall not eat, for in the day that you eat of it you shall surely die."

Key References

"Image" (1:26): This is the Hebrew word *tselem*, which means "a resembling figure or image." Later in the Old Testament, this word is translated as "idol" to describe a physical depiction of a deity. The word "icon" could also be used to define what *tselem* means. Put simply, humans in God's story are icons, little representatives of God on earth. Idols are denounced later in the Old Testament because God has already set up icons of himself everywhere: human beings!

"Likeness" (1:26): This is the Hebrew word *demuth*, which can mean "resembles," "of the same fashion," and "similitude." This word is used in Genesis 5:3 to describe how Seth resembles his father, Adam. Not only are humans little icons of God throughout creation representing him, but humans also *reflect* God, just as children reflect their parents.

"Dominion" (1:26, 28): This word has been misunderstood throughout the centuries. The word can have the connotation of "domination" or "mastery," which can become a license for some to exploit the resources of God's creation toward their own ends. However, it is interesting to note that the next time this word is used comes in Leviticus 25, which contains the instructions on how Israel is to celebrate the year of Jubilee. In this context, God asks his people not to rule harshly over those who are in some form of physical or economic bondage but rather to show care and generosity during the Jubilee years. In short, dominion in the context of God's character means faithful stewardship and cultivation of every part of God's world.

Reflect

The aim of this section is for you to dialogue as a group about what insights and questions come to mind as you hear God's Word. Use the discussion questions below to guide the conversation.

- What do you think it means to be made in the "image" and "likeness" of someone?

- In your own words, how would you define the term "dominion" used in Genesis 1:26, 28? What do you think it means for humans today to have dominion over God's world? Where have you experienced good dominion?

- After God blessed the first humans, what did he invite them to do, and what did he invite them to enjoy?

- In Genesis 2:15, the phrase "work [the garden]" could also be translated as "to cultivate." As you think about your current work, what do you cultivate or form?

- Imagine for a moment that you didn't know sin would enter into the world in God's story. What do you think the garden of Eden would have been like if the first humans had centuries to cultivate and take care of it in God's presence? Paint a picture together.

Respond

The goal of this Bible study is not to create anxious activity but *prayerful response* to what God is revealing to you. Each week, there will be a practical way for you to respond to what you are learning that is directly related to your work.

Gratitude journal

The invitation this week is to start a gratitude journal for your work.

- As you go about your work this week, expect to notice moments of truth, goodness, and beauty. This might take some deep reflection in difficult workplaces. Be open to being surprised.

- Write these moments down as you encounter them.

- The goal is to develop a list of ten moments of gratitude from your workweek.

- Be prepared to bring a few of these moments to share with your group next week.

- You can use either a printed journal or a digital note for quick reference.

Release

See the ending of each week together as a release into God's world for the good work he has called us to. Stand and recite this commissioning together each week:

God, you have made us in your image to care and cultivate your good creation.

However, we recognize our work is filled with thorns and thistles, injustice and mistreatment.

The world is not the way it is supposed to be.

Yet you have not abandoned your world, but through Jesus Christ you have sprouted forth seeds of new creation everywhere we look.

Holy Spirit, breath of the living God, send us now as partners with Christ into every industry to demonstrate and declare good news until Christ's return.

Notes

Week One

Leader's Notes

Reflect

What do you think it means to be made in the "image" and "likeness" of someone?

Help the group see that the image is much like a child reflecting the features of their parents. Likeness, however, communicates more than reflecting; it means that humans represent God in the world. Reflecting and representing God is the calling of humans everywhere, especially in their work.

In your own words, how would you define the term "dominion" used in Genesis 1:26, 28? What do you think it means for humans today to have dominion over God's world? Where have you experienced good dominion?

Help your group develop a working definition of dominion. The temptation might be to quickly jump to broken examples of dominion, but gently help your group return to good examples of dominion. (We will explore how sin has distorted our work next week.)

After God blessed the first humans, what did he invite them to do, and what did he invite them to enjoy?

Lead the discussion toward what is said in Genesis 1:28–30. God invited them to be fruitful, increase in number, fill the earth, subdue the earth, have dominion over the creatures of the earth, and enjoy the vegetation of the earth for food.

In Genesis 2:15, the phrase "work [the garden]" could also be translated as "to cultivate." As you think about your current work, what do you cultivate or form?

This might be a challenging question for some people in your group. As people share what they do for their work, have the other participants help them identify what they cultivate and form. See this time as a moment of encouragement for people to see that their work matters.

Imagine for a moment that you didn't know sin would enter into the world in God's story. What do you think the garden of Eden would have been like if the first humans had centuries to cultivate and take care of it in God's presence? Paint a picture together.

The goal of this question is to spark imagination for what the world would be like without sin. Many people imagine the garden of Eden as a finished product rather than an ongoing project of development with God. Help your group imagine what the garden of Eden would have become over centuries of stewardship. What stories of flourishing would be told?

Week
Two

The Distortion
of Work

Introduction

Tragedy strikes. The beautiful and intricate work of God in Genesis 1 and 2 becomes contaminated by Genesis 3. An upward trajectory of human flourishing, development, and unbelievable potential has now been redirected into a downward spiral caused by human sin. Sin's corrosive nature is especially displayed in Genesis 11 during the construction of the Tower of Babel. The first humans were given an incredible vocational assignment to be fruitful, multiply, and exercise loving dominion; but by Genesis 11, humanity has shredded the original design and replaced it with an idea of their own. Now, they gather to build a tower high enough to reach God so that they may make a name for themselves (Genesis 11:4). In their book *The Drama of Scripture*, Craig Bartholomew and Michael Goheen say, "Babel is a monumental, communal attempt by Adam's race to wrest human autonomy from God once more."[1]

The Tower of Babel went on to become an icon for cities that stand in opposition to God. But for the purposes of this guide, Babel can also be seen as a clear example of the distortion of work. The story gives us at least three insights into how sin has infected our work:

1. **Wielding new technologies in distorted ways (Genesis 11:3).** Notice how the humans use a new technology for the ancient world (baking bricks) to build this city in opposition to God. In a variety of vocational spheres and industries today, the wielding of new technologies for questionable purposes is rampant. Whether it is related to the creation of powerful algorithms, developing devices that create compulsive patterns, or using social media to bully and marginalize others, humans have an incredible capacity to take good technological advancements and distort them.

2. **Believing "good ends" justify questionable means (Genesis 11:4a).** It could be commendable that the humans of this story desire to get closer to the heavens, possibly to have an encounter with God. Humans were designed to have a relationship with God, after all. However, the *means* of obtaining this are questionable and in contrast with how God had interacted with the human race so far. The story of Scripture is one of God coming down to us rather than us ascending to God's level. When it comes to our work, there is a temptation to believe "good" ends justify questionable means.

3. **Creating our own identity rather than receiving it from God (Genesis 11:4).** The fundamental flaw of the project of Babel is that humans attempt to create a new identity for themselves instead of receiving the one they already had. In verse 4, they say, "Let us make a name for ourselves." But the reality is that humans were already made in God's image and likeness. They already had a name and an identity—the very identity of being a partner with God! Workplaces often become places where we attempt to make a name for ourselves through competition and leveraging.

Let's explore how this story of Genesis 11 might create an opportunity for repentance and renewal for your group.

---

[1] Craig G. Bartholemew and Michael W. Goheen, *The Drama of Scripture: Finding Our Place in the Biblical Story,* Second Edition (Grand Rapids, MI: Baker Academic, 2014), 50.

Ready

The unbelievable truth is this: You are about to hear God speak. Every time you pick up the Bible, an encounter with God is possible. First, ready yourself to enter God's presence and hear his voice. To begin, offer this simple prayer to God and then wait in silence for two minutes:

Father, help me hear your voice.
Jesus, help me sense your presence.
Spirit, help me live according to your ways.

Read

After sitting in silence for two minutes, choose someone to read the passage below. Then choose a different person to read through the passage again.

Genesis 11:1–9:

[1] Now the whole earth had one language and the same words. [2] And as people migrated **from the east**, they found a plain in the land of Shinar and settled there. [3] And they said to one another, "Come, let us **make bricks, and burn them** thoroughly." And they had brick for stone, and bitumen for mortar. [4] Then they said, "Come, let us **build ourselves a city and a tower** with its top in the heavens, and let us make a name for ourselves, lest we be dispersed over the face of the whole earth." [5] And the LORD came down to see the city and the tower, which the children of man had built. [6] And the LORD said, "Behold, they are one people, and they have all one language, and this is only the beginning of what they will do. And nothing that they propose to do will now be impossible for them. [7] Come, let us go down and there confuse their language, so that they may not understand one another's speech." [8] So the LORD dispersed them from there over the face of all the earth, and they left off building the city. [9] Therefore its name was called Babel, because there the LORD confused the language of all the earth. And from there the LORD dispersed them over the face of all the earth.

Key References

"From the east" (11:2): This is a literary pattern in the early chapters of Genesis to indicate a growing autonomy from God. Adam and Eve traveled east out of the garden (Genesis 3:24). Cain went away from the presence of the Lord and traveled east of Eden (4:16). And now people are migrating east in this story in pending rebellion against God (11:2). Later in Genesis, Lot journeys east away from Abraham (13:11).

"Make bricks, and burn them" (11:3): The work of "baking bricks" was an emerging new technology for building sturdy and water-resistant external structures for buildings.

"Build ourselves a city and a tower" (11:4): The tower being referred to here was most likely what ancients would call a *ziggurat*. Towers like these were crafted to create a stairway to heaven, where it was believed the gods lived. In other words, this would be a place where heaven and earth supposedly met. The builders of Babel similarly may have believed that the top of the tower would be a "gate" into God's presence.

Reflect

The aim of this section is for you to dialogue as a group about what insights and questions come to mind as you hear God's Word. Use the discussion questions below to guide the conversation.

- As you heard the story of the Tower of Babel, what details grabbed your attention?

- Since Adam and Eve sinned in Genesis 3, how did humans continue to rebel against God up to this point in the story in Genesis 11? Give some examples. How has work specifically been distorted in these stories?

- It says that the people used a new technology: making bricks and burning them thoroughly. This was a new way of building in the ancient world. Think about technology in your industry and workplace. How have new technologies served your industry well or in ways that are redemptive? How have you seen new technologies used in questionable ways? How have you witnessed questionable means being justified with "good ends"?

- What do you think it means that the humans at Babel wanted to make a name for themselves? How do you see this play out in your workplace? What about in different industries?

- Why do you think God came down, confused their language, and scattered the people?

Respond

The goal of this Bible study is not to create anxious activity but *prayerful response* to what God is revealing to you. Each week, there will be a practical way for you to respond to what you are learning that is directly related to your work.

Brokenness journal

The invitation this week is to start a brokenness journal for your work.

- As you go about your work this week, ask the Holy Spirit to reveal areas where your work and industry have been distorted by sin. Remember, sin isn't just the personal decisions people might make in your workplace. Sin also causes broken relationships, communities, and entire systems.

- Write these areas down as you notice them this week.

- The goal is to develop a list of ten areas of brokenness from your workweek.

- Be prepared to bring a few of these areas to share with your group next week.

- You can use either a printed journal or a digital note for quick reference.

Release

See the ending of each week together as a release into God's world for the good work he has called us to. Stand and recite this commissioning together each week:

God, you have made us in your image to care and cultivate your good creation.

However, we recognize our work is filled with thorns and thistles, injustice and mistreatment.

The world is not the way it is supposed to be.

Yet you have not abandoned your world, but through Jesus Christ you have sprouted forth seeds of new creation everywhere we look.

Holy Spirit, breath of the living God, send us now as partners with Christ into every industry to demonstrate and declare good news until Christ's return.

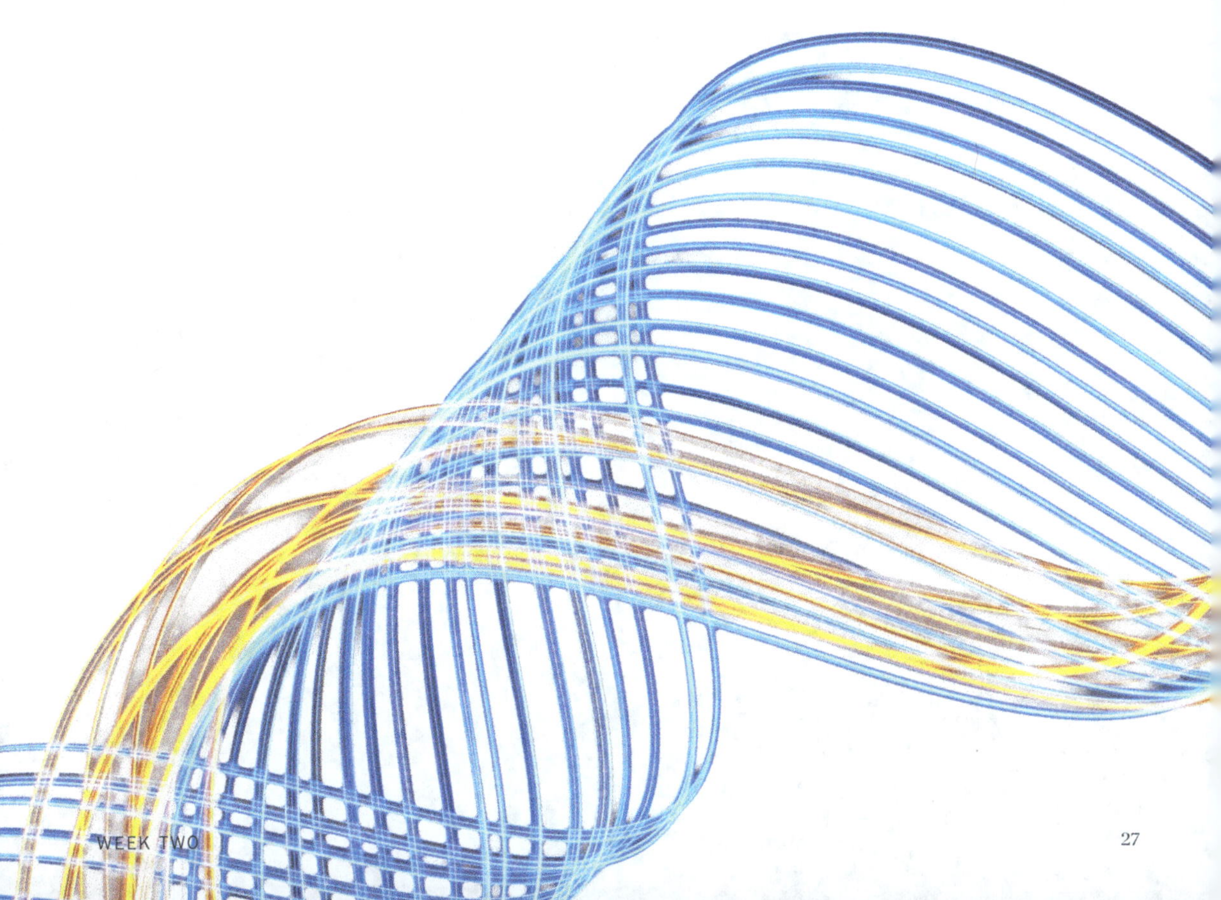

Notes

Week Two

Leader's Notes

Reflect

As you heard the story of the Tower of Babel, what details grabbed your attention?

The goal of this question is to create curiosity and dialogue. This is an ancient story that can be difficult to understand, and not every question in this session will be answered thoroughly. The desired outcome is to invite self-exploration and learn how this story might relate to the existing distortion of work.

Since Adam and Eve sinned in Genesis 3, how did humans continue to rebel against God up to this point in the story in Genesis 11? Give some examples. How has work specifically been distorted in these stories?

Genesis 11 is a low point in a downward spiral of sin. Encourage participants to trace the story of sin so far from Genesis 3–11 and notice how work has been distorted since the original mandate of being fruitful, multiplying, and exercising dominion. Examples that could be shared are: the ground has now been cursed because of sin; murder and violence are the antithesis of being fruitful and multiplying; Noah cultivates a vineyard only to get drunk on its fruit; and instead of filling the earth, humans are congregating in one location at Babel.

It says that the people used a new technology: making bricks and burning them thoroughly. This was a new way of building in the ancient world. Think about technology in your industry and workplace. How have new technologies served your industry well or in ways that are redemptive? How have you seen new technologies used in questionable ways? How have you witnessed questionable means being justified with "good ends"?

This question is to help people explore how the infiltration of new technologies into all of human life might promise incredible advancements and productivity, but also have overlooked side effects. Help people see technology as neither entirely good nor utterly evil, but as a tool that can be wielded in a variety of beneficial or harmful ways in their work.

What do you think it means that the humans at Babel wanted to make a name for themselves? How do you see this play out in your workplace? What about in different industries?

Try to get people to put what they think this might mean into their own words. The goal is to facilitate the conversation toward seeing this crafting of their own name as an act of pride and autonomy from a God who had already given them one. Names in the ancient world were the most powerful signifier of identity.

Why do you think God came down, confused their language, and scattered the people?

The simple truth is that humans weren't participating in his commission to fill the earth and have dominion over it.

Week Three

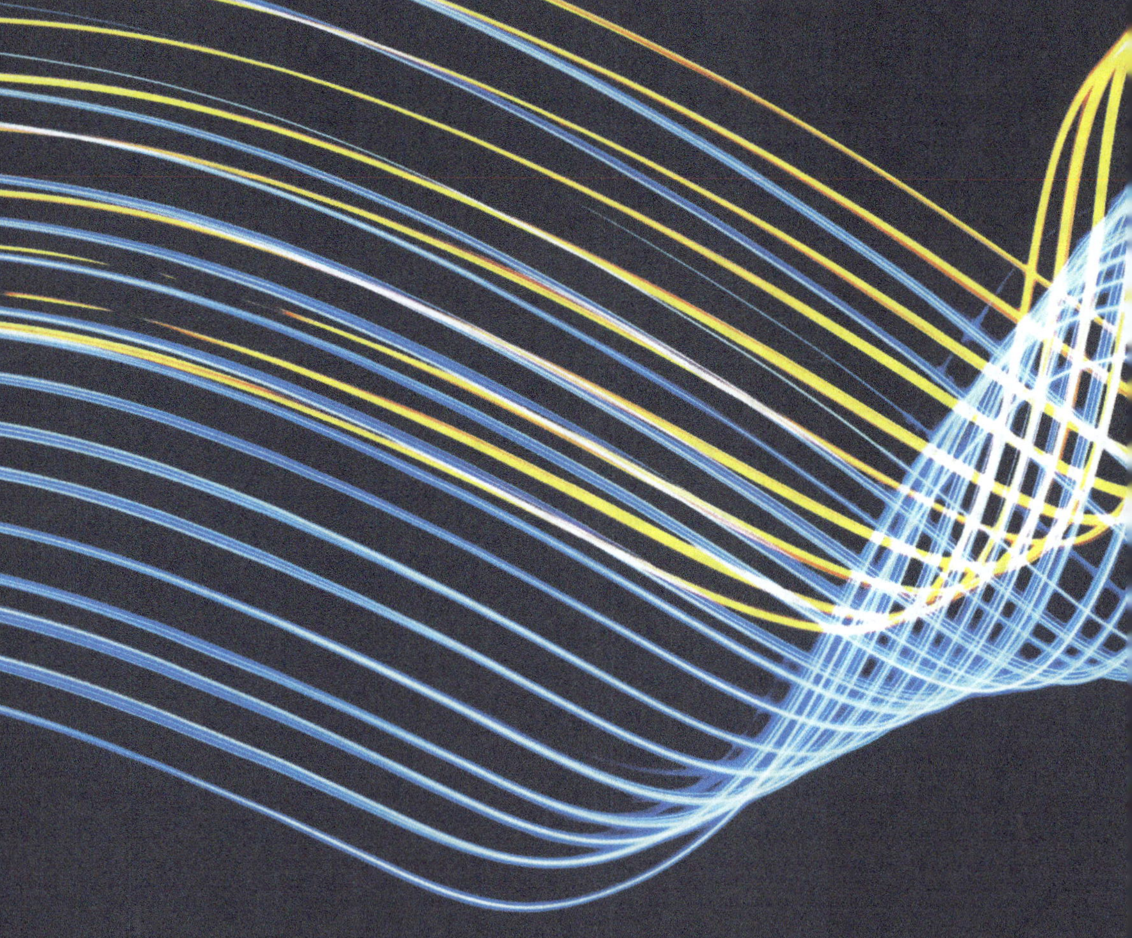

The Call to Mission

Introduction

The downward spiral of sin, brokenness, and rebellion reaches a climax at the Tower of Babel. As Genesis 11 closes, the reader is left with two gnawing questions: Has God forsaken his creation? Is the story over?

Thankfully, things are far from finished. A reversal takes place. Instead of humans reaching the heavens through a tower, God comes to humanity by appearing to Abram (later Abraham). Genesis 12 sets a new pathway for humanity and all of creation, as God promises that through Abram all the nations of the earth will be blessed (Genesis 12:3). God loves his creation too much to abandon it. In this part of the story, the primary way blessing flows to the nations is through God's people—the Israelites—embodying who God is by the way they live as a distinct people.

This calling had its challenges. Hundreds of years after Abraham, the people of God found themselves enslaved in Egypt under another god: Pharaoh. But God hears the cries of his people and brings about their deliverance. As the Israelites stand on the precipice of a new chapter in their history, God clarifies their calling as a people in Exodus 19:1–6.

What does he call them? *Treasured possession. Kingdom of priests. Holy nation.* These are the powerful identity markers God gives his vulnerable people journeying through the wilderness to the Promised Land. In short, God's people are to mediate for the nations the very presence of God.

With this identity in mind, our work, whether it is paid or unpaid, becomes a primary avenue for people to encounter the gospel and be transformed by the kindness of God.

Ready

The unbelievable truth is this: You are about to hear God speak. Every time you pick up the Bible, an encounter with God is possible. First, ready yourself to enter God's presence and hear his voice. To begin, offer this simple prayer to God and then wait in silence for two minutes:

Father, help me hear your voice.
Jesus, help me sense your presence.
Spirit, help me live according to your ways.

Read

After sitting in silence for two minutes, choose someone to read the passage below. Then choose a different person to read through the passage again.

Exodus 19:1–6:

[1]**On the third new moon** after the people of Israel had gone out of the land of Egypt, on that day they came into the wilderness of Sinai. [2]They set out from Rephidim and came into the wilderness of Sinai, and they encamped in the wilderness. There Israel encamped before the mountain, [3]while Moses went up to God. The LORD called to him out of the mountain, saying, "Thus you shall say to the house of Jacob, and tell the people of Israel: [4]'You yourselves have seen what I did to the Egyptians, and how I bore you on **eagles' wings** and brought you to myself. [5] Now therefore, if you will indeed obey my voice and **keep my covenant**, you shall be my treasured possession among all peoples, for all the earth is mine; [6]and you shall be to me a **kingdom of priests and a holy nation**.' These are the words that you shall speak to the people of Israel."

Key References

"On the third new moon" (19:1): This simply means that it has been three months since Israel was miraculously delivered out of Egypt and across the Red Sea.

"Eagles' wings" (19:4): This is a metaphor that will be used throughout the Old Testament as a picture of God's care and deliverance of his people. It is most extensively explained in Deuteronomy 32:10–11: "He found him in a desert land, and in the howling waste of the wilderness; he encircled him, he cared for him, he kept him as the apple of his eye. Like an eagle that stirs up its nest, that flutters over its young, spreading out its wings, catching them, bearing them on its pinions." Another passage where this imagery is used is Isaiah 40:31: "They shall mount up with wings like eagles."

"Keep my covenant" (19:5): This is a reference to the covenant God made with Abraham (Genesis 15:18; Genesis 17:1–21).

"Kingdom of priests and a holy nation" (19:6): The Hebrew word for holy is *qadosh*, which means to be "set apart" or "distinct." Like God, Israel is to be a distinct people from the surrounding nations. However, this distinction is not for the intention of isolation from the world but for the sake of being able to bless the world. This is why "holy nation" is also paired with "kingdom of priests," as Israel is to be a mediator of God's grace to everyone they come in contact with.

Reflect

The aim of this section is for you to dialogue as a group about what insights and questions come to mind as you hear God's Word. Use the discussion questions below to guide the conversation.

- As you heard the passage from Exodus 19:1–6, did you sense God grabbing your attention with a certain phrase or moment in the story?

- As you heard the identity markers God gives his people in this passage (treasured possession, kingdom of priests, holy nation), which one most resonated with you?

- 1 Peter 2:9–11 reaffirms that Christians carry these identity markers in light of Jesus' death and resurrection. Share with your group in what ways you are a mediator of God's presence in your workplace. Try to think through specific examples.

Spend some time praying for each person in your group to fully live into the identity God has given them. Pray that they become a bridge of the gospel in their workplace this year.

Respond

The goal of this Bible study is not to create anxious activity but *prayerful response* to what God is revealing to each person. Each week, there will be a practical way for you to respond to what you are learning that is directly related to your work.

BLESS rhythms

The invitation this week is to practice the BLESS rhythms in your workplaces. BLESS is an acronym for *Bless, Listen, Eat, Speak, and Sabbath*. Consider focusing on one rhythm for each of the next five days. Here are potential questions to answer for each rhythm this week:

- **Bless:** Who can I tangibly bless today in word or deed in my workplace?

- **Listen:** Who can I listen to in my workplace who is potentially overlooked?

- **Eat:** Who can I share a meal with who I typically don't interact with?

- **Speak:** Who can I encourage and potentially connect their work to God's mission in my workplace?

- **Sabbath:** Who can I invite into a practice of rest that I am planning in the coming week?

Release

See the ending of each week together as a release into God's world for the good work he has called us to. Stand and recite this commissioning together each week:

God, you have made us in your image to care and cultivate your good creation.

However, we recognize our work is filled with thorns and thistles, injustice and mistreatment.

The world is not the way it is supposed to be.

Yet you have not abandoned your world, but through Jesus Christ you have sprouted forth seeds of new creation everywhere we look.

Holy Spirit, breath of the living God, send us now as partners with Christ into every industry to demonstrate and declare good news until Christ's return.

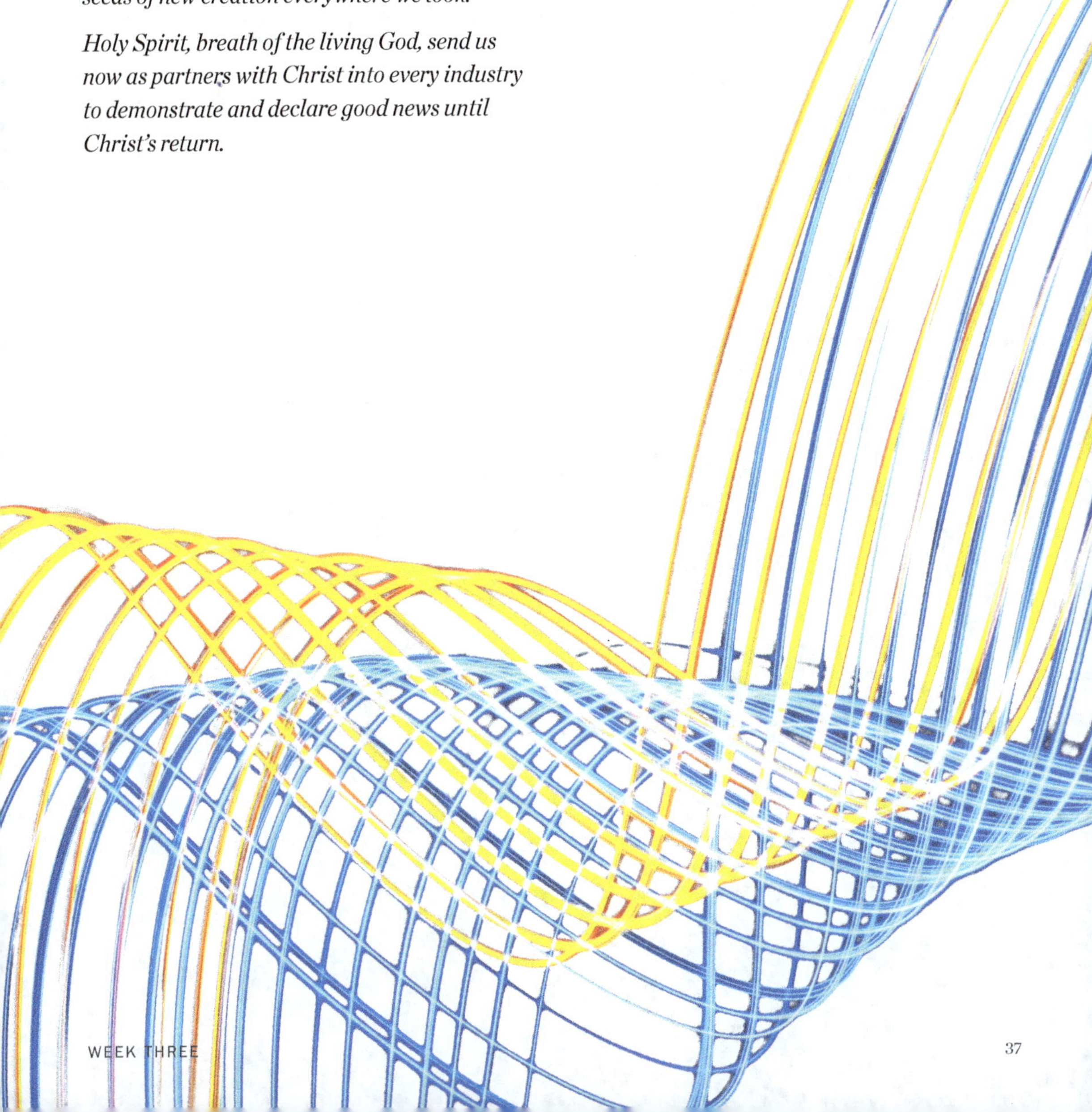

Notes

Week Three

Leader's Notes

Reflect

As you heard the passage from Exodus 19:1–6, did you sense God grabbing your attention with a certain phrase or moment in the story?

The goal of this question is to create an open dialogue, allowing the Holy Spirit to speak and illuminate the text to your group.

As you heard the identity markers God gives his people in this passage (treasured possession, kingdom of priests, holy nation), which one most resonated with you?

Help your group see these identity markers as not just for God's people in the past but for them, as well.

1 Peter 2:9–11 reaffirms that Christians carry these identity markers in light of Jesus' death and resurrection. Share with your group in what ways you are a mediator of God's presence in your workplace. Try to think through specific examples.

Lead your group to identify concrete ways they are mediators of God's grace in and through their work. Areas of conversation could include the way they do their work, how their work contributes to the flourishing of others, and opportunities they have had to share with their coworkers about how their work connects with the gospel.

Example: A transit worker in NYC can be a mediator of God's presence by creating a clean environment for public transport and preventing the spread of viruses. They are also a mediator of God's presence by monitoring the safety of travel whether by driving or designing the path the vehicle will move on.

Another example: Because God cares for those at the margins, someone in the finance industry can mediate God's presence by providing equitable capital for those who have the desire and competencies to start a thriving business but are overlooked or vulnerable. Because God is for justice and tells the truth, another way someone in finance could mediate God's presence is through accurate accounting and fair interest.

Week
Four

The Impact
of Idols

Introduction

The powerful speech God gives his people in Exodus 19 ended with the Israelites responding with, "All that the Lᴏʀᴅ has spoken we will do" (v. 8). But unfortunately, they did not. By chapter 32, the people of God become impatient with the pace of God. As Moses is receiving the Ten Commandments on Mount Sinai, an anxious mob of Israelites come to Aaron demanding new gods be fashioned. Instead of resisting the people, Aaron caves in to their demands.

Just one chapter earlier, the Spirit of God filled Bezalel with wisdom, knowledge, and all kinds of skills to be a craftsman of a variety of materials (Exodus 31:1–5). But now, the skill of a craftsman becomes an avenue for idolatry in the hands of Aaron. The mission God's people were tasked with has been sabotaged.

This chaos and rebellion cause God to briefly reimagine his plan to bless the world through Israel and instead to restart with Moses. But Moses pleads with God to relent of his anger, and God resists destroying the entire nation despite their rebellion. Moses' mediation on behalf of God's people becomes an icon of the true and better Moses (Hebrews 3:1–6) who is to come and who will satisfy the wrath of God on our behalf at the cross: Jesus.

Empowered by the Holy Spirit, our work has the incredible capacity to be for the flourishing of all. But it also has the capacity to be an instrument of idolatry and the worship of false gods. Idolatry is when we take the good things of God's creation and make them *ultimate* things. It's when we look to somewhere, something, someone, or some experience as the solution to our restless, anxious hearts.

Ready

The unbelievable truth is this: You are about to hear God speak. Every time you pick up the Bible, an encounter with God is possible. First, ready yourself to enter God's presence and hear his voice. To begin, offer this simple prayer to God and then wait in silence for two minutes:

Father, help me hear your voice.
Jesus, help me sense your presence.
Spirit, help me live according to your ways.

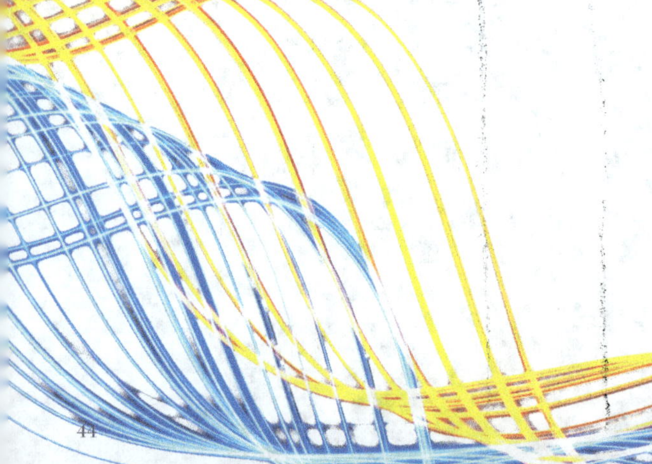

Read

After sitting in silence for two minutes, choose someone to read the passage below. Then choose a different person to read through the passage again.

Exodus 32:1-14:

[1] When the people saw that Moses delayed to come down from the mountain, the people gathered themselves together to Aaron and said to him, "Up, make us gods who shall go before us. As for this Moses, the man who brought us up out of the land of Egypt, we do not know what has become of him." [2] So Aaron said to them, "Take off the **rings of gold** that are in the ears of your wives, your sons, and your daughters, and bring them to me." [3] So all the people took off the rings of gold that were in their ears and brought them to Aaron. [4] And he received the gold from their hand and fashioned it with a graving tool and made a golden calf. And they said, "These are your gods, O Israel, who brought you up out of the land of Egypt!" [5] When Aaron saw this, he built an altar before it. And Aaron made a proclamation and said, "Tomorrow shall be a feast to the LORD." [6] And they rose up early the next day and offered burnt offerings and brought peace offerings. And the people sat down to eat and drink and rose up to play.

[7] And the LORD said to Moses, "Go down, for your people, whom you brought up out of the land of Egypt, have corrupted themselves. [8] They have turned aside quickly out of the way that I commanded them. They have made for themselves **a golden calf** and have worshiped it and sacrificed to it and said, 'These are your gods, O Israel, who brought you up out of the land of Egypt!'" [9] And the LORD said to Moses, "I have seen this people, and behold, it is a stiff-necked people. [10] Now therefore let me alone, that my wrath may burn hot against them and I may consume them, in order that I may make a great nation of you."

[11] But Moses implored the LORD his God and said, "O LORD, why does your wrath burn hot against your people, whom you have brought out of the land of Egypt with great power and with a mighty hand? [12] Why should the Egyptians say, 'With evil intent did he bring them out, to kill them in the mountains and to consume them from the face of the earth'? Turn from your burning anger and relent from this disaster against your people. [13] **Remember Abraham, Isaac, and Israel**, your servants, to whom you swore by your own self, and said to them, 'I will multiply your offspring as the stars of heaven, and all this land that I have promised I will give to your offspring, and they shall inherit it forever.'" [14] And the LORD relented from the disaster that he had spoken of bringing on his people.

Key References

"Rings of gold" (32:2): Where did this gold come from? Likely, the gold that Aaron is asking for was from Egypt. As Israel exited the country, God commissioned the people to ask for gold and silver from the Egyptians (Exodus 11:2; 12:35). These metals, which were a tangible picture of God's deliverance, are now exploited for rebellion and idolatry.

"A golden calf" (32:8): This is another way to say a "young bull," which would have been an ancient symbol of power and fertility.

"Remember Abraham, Isaac, and Israel" (32:13): Moses pleads with God to remember the covenant he made with Abraham's family starting in Genesis 12:1–3. God will not forsake his promise because it was made not only for Israel but also for the entire world. If Israel was destroyed, the nations would lose the conduit in which blessing would one day flow to them through the faithful and true Israelite: Jesus of Nazareth (John 1:47).

Reflect

The aim of this section is for you to dialogue as a group about what insights and questions come to mind as you hear God's Word. Use the discussion questions below to guide the conversation.

- Why do you think the people became impatient with God and his messenger, Moses?

- Do you resonate with Aaron? Have you found yourself reluctantly participating in the sin of others because it feels too great, costly, or dangerous to resist? How have you seen this dynamic play out in your workplace?

- The golden calf was a symbol of power and fertility. In what ways have you experienced people in your workplace looking to power and strength as their god? Could you identify the key idols of your industry?

- In this story, how does Moses foreshadow Jesus? What parallels do you see?

Respond

The goal of this Bible study is not to create anxious activity but *prayerful response* to what God is revealing to you. Each week, there will be a practical way for you to respond to what you are learning that is directly related to your work.

Heart idolatry journal

The invitation this week is to unearth heart idols at work and apply the gospel to your deepest being. You will do this by journaling your reflections over the week. A helpful illustration of how idols function is to imagine you are about to go for a swim, but you spot a shark's fin poking out of the water. The reason you wouldn't venture into the water is not the fin itself but what the fin represents underneath the surface—a giant shark! This is how idolatry functions in our lives. There is a sinful behavior on the surface (a surface idol) that manifests in our lives, but underneath that behavior is a deeper motivation (a deep idol) that drives our decisions. For us to experience heart renewal, we need to not only name what is happening on the surface but uncover our motivations as well.

Luke 6:43–45:

[43] "For no good tree bears bad fruit, nor again does a bad tree bear good fruit, [44] for each tree is known by its own fruit. For figs are not gathered from thornbushes, nor are grapes picked from a bramble bush. [45] The good person out of the good treasure of his heart produces good, and the evil person out of his evil treasure produces evil, for out of the abundance of the heart his mouth speaks."

An example

Let's explore how deep idols are unearthed with two examples.

First, imagine you are working on a project with a coworker in your department. It has taken months to put the project together, organize the key findings, and create a presentation to share your insights with the larger company. Your partner ends up being the primary voice in the presentation, and in the conversations that follow, you repeatedly hear how this was "his" project while your name rarely gets mentioned. He experiences praise while you are overlooked. You become angry and frustrated that you aren't getting the recognition you rightfully deserve. As you explore your motivations, a deep idol begins to emerge underneath the anger: approval. You desire the approval of others so much that in this situation you felt crushed because you weren't being recognized.

Second, imagine your primary vocational calling in this season is as a father or a mother while your spouse works outside the home. As a parent, you carefully plan each week for your children as you seek to cultivate their hearts in the kingdom of God and give them a beautiful picture of Jesus. One day, you are at a nearby park with your kids, and you see a neighbor with their kids, as well. As the kids are playing and having fun, you see one of your kids shove the neighbor's child down the slide and laugh. As you seek to correct your child, they begin screaming at you—which now has the attention of everyone. On the surface, you are deeply disappointed by your kid's behavior and treat them more harshly than necessary. In the moment, you are frustrated because you have been diligent in teaching them how to treat others respectfully, and yet they haven't lived by that instruction. Later, as you reflect on the moment, a deep idol emerges: control. You were operating under the false belief that if you do everything right as a parent, your child will always do the right thing—you will be able to control the outcomes of your child's life.

Journal questions

- As you think about this season of your life and work, what surface idols do you notice?

- Are you able to trace your surface idols to the deeper idols of your heart?

- As you reflect, do you believe control, approval, comfort, success, or security is the primary motivator of your decisions?

- As you name some of the idols of your heart, what emotions come up for you?

- Another way to think about idolatry would be to complete this sentence: Jesus + _______ = happiness. The blank represents the idol we hold. How would you complete that sentence in this season?

Release

See the ending of each week together as a release into God's world for the good work he has called us to. Stand and recite this commissioning together each week:

God, you have made us in your image to care and cultivate your good creation.

However, we recognize our work is filled with thorns and thistles, injustice and mistreatment.

The world is not the way it is supposed to be.

Yet you have not abandoned your world, but through Jesus Christ you have sprouted forth seeds of new creation everywhere we look.

Holy Spirit, breath of the living God, send us now as partners with Christ into every industry to demonstrate and declare good news until Christ's return.

Notes

Week Four

Leader's Notes

Reflect

Why do you think the people became impatient with God and his messenger, Moses?

This question helps people enter into the story and the characters involved.

Do you resonate with Aaron? Have you found yourself reluctantly participating in the sin of others because it feels too great, costly, or dangerous to resist? How have you seen this dynamic play out in your workplace?

Aaron was a reluctant participant in the sin of God's people. Yet he allowed their anxiety to lead him to create an idolatrous image. Encourage people to resonate with Aaron's predicament and then lead the conversation to how this pattern might play out in their workplace.

The golden calf was a symbol of power and fertility. In what ways have you experienced people in your workplace looking to power and strength as their god? Could you identify the key idols of your industry?

The aim here is to get people thinking about their workplace from the context of idolatry. What are the things people in every workplace orient their affection and attention around?

In this story, how does Moses foreshadow Jesus? What parallels do you see?

The goal here is to help people see Jesus as the true and better Moses who took on the wrath of God and mediated on behalf of God's people so they might not receive destruction but deliverance through the cross and resurrection.

Week Five

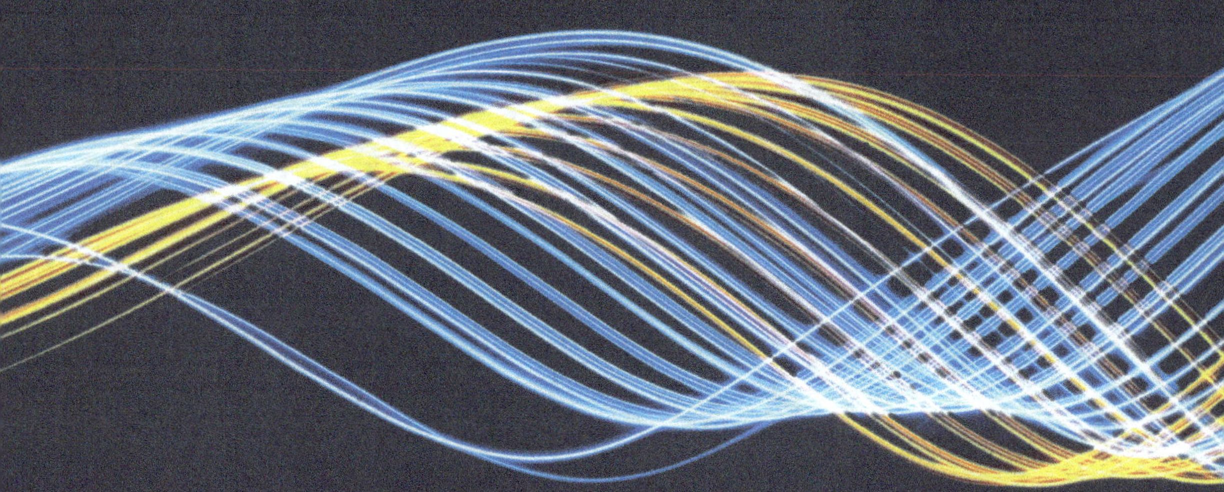

What Mission
Looks Like
(MARK 5:21–43)

Introduction

We have been exploring how our work is integral to the mission and witness of God in the world. Through this study, you have been invited to reimagine your workplace as an avenue to the gospel in people's lives. What exciting news! God desires for you to see how his kingdom is breaking through wherever you already are and whatever you're already doing. This week, the goal is to begin developing a picture of what the mission of God might look like through our work. To do this, we will look to Jesus.

Every encounter Jesus has in the Gospels is both an invitation for us to imagine ourselves as the recipients of his grace, as well as an opportunity to see Jesus as an example of how we should treat others. Today, we are going to explore Mark 5:21–43 and focus on Jesus' relationship with the hemorrhaging woman.

Ready

The unbelievable truth is this: You are about to hear God speak. Every time you pick up the Bible, an encounter with God is possible. First, ready yourself to enter God's presence and hear his voice. To begin, offer this simple prayer to God and then wait in silence for two minutes:

Father, help me hear your voice.
Jesus, help me sense your presence.
Spirit, help me live according to your ways.

Read

After sitting in silence for two minutes, choose someone to read the passage below. Then choose a different person to read through the passage again.

Mark 5:21–43:

21 And when Jesus had **crossed** again in the boat to the other side, a great crowd gathered about him, and he was beside the sea. 22 Then came one of the rulers of the synagogue, **Jairus** by name, and seeing him, he fell at his feet 23 and implored him earnestly, saying, "My little daughter is at the point of death. Come and lay your hands on her, so that she may be made well and live." 24 And he went with him.

And a great crowd followed him and thronged about him. 25 **And there was a woman** who had had a discharge of blood for twelve years, 26 and who had suffered much under many physicians, and had spent all that she had, and was no better but rather grew worse. 27 She had heard the reports about Jesus and came up behind him in the crowd and **touched his garment**. 28 For she said, "If I touch even his garments, I will be made well." 29 And immediately the flow of blood dried up, and she felt in her body that she was healed of her disease. 30 And Jesus, perceiving in himself that power had gone out from him, immediately turned about in the crowd and said, "Who touched my garments?" [31] And his disciples said to him, "You see the crowd pressing around you, and **yet you say, 'Who touched me?'**" [32] And he looked around to see who had done it. [33] But the woman, knowing what had happened to her, came in fear and trembling and fell down before him and told him the whole truth. [34] And he said to her, "**Daughter, your faith has made you well**; go in peace, and be healed of your disease."

[35] While he was still speaking, there came from the ruler's house some who said, "Your daughter is dead. Why trouble the Teacher any further?" [36] But overhearing what they said, Jesus said to the ruler of the synagogue, "Do not fear, only believe." [37] And he allowed no one to follow him except Peter and James and John the brother of James. [38] They came to the house of the ruler of the synagogue, and Jesus saw a commotion, people weeping and wailing loudly. [39] And when he had entered, he said to them, "Why are you making a commotion and weeping? The child is not dead but sleeping." [40] And they laughed at him. But he put them all outside and took the child's father and mother and those who were with him and went in where the child was. [41] Taking her by the hand he said to her, "Talitha cumi," which means, "Little girl, I say to you, arise." [42] And immediately the girl got up and began walking (for she was twelve years of age), and they were immediately overcome with amazement. [43] And he strictly charged them that no one should know this, and told them to give her something to eat.

Key References

"Crossed" (5:21): This is a detail easily overlooked. In the previous story, Jesus crossed into a Gentile region and healed the demoniac (Mark 5:1–20). Now, he crosses back into Jewish territory before this new encounter. The kingdom of God has come for all peoples in all places, and Mark is showcasing that to us in this chapter.

"Jairus" (5:22): The first key character of the story is introduced. It should be noted that a "synagogue leader" was a person of prestige and power. Yet, he comes kneeling before Jesus. The insight here is that both the powerful (Jairus) and the poor (woman) need the kingdom of God to break through.

"And there was a woman" (5:25): This woman is having a multifaceted experience of suffering. First, she is experiencing horrible physical pain from her twelve years of bleeding. Second, she is experiencing the despair of looking to doctors for solutions, only to find nothing. But a third aspect of suffering that is potentially overlooked by Western readers is that this woman is experiencing social isolation and shame because her condition makes her unclean and unfit to participate in the community due to Levitical law.

"Touched his garment" (5:27): It was a common belief that the cloak of a religious healer could have a supernatural effect and produce healing. Hence, the woman attempts to touch Jesus' cloak.

"Yet you say, 'Who touched me?'" (5:31): The disciples' response here is normative for them. They are often unaware in the moment of what Jesus is up to. Notice how Jesus sees the interruption along the way to Jairus's daughter not as a nuisance but as a divine appointment for God to show up.

"Daughter, your faith has made you well" (5:34): This woman has experienced enough shame. Why doesn't Jesus just let the woman go on her way unnoticed in the crowd? Because Jesus understands that this woman not only needs physical healing but also social healing and welcoming back into the community. By giving her this new identity of "daughter" in front of the community, she is able to experience holistic healing!

Reflect

The aim of this section is for you to dialogue as a group about what insights and questions come to mind as you hear God's Word. Use the discussion questions below to guide the conversation.

- As you heard the story, what detail, phrase, or moment did the Holy Spirit use to grab your attention?

- Do you resonate more with Jairus or the woman in this story? Why?

- As you watch Jesus respond to the situation unfolding, what insights do you glean about the mission of God?

- How might this story shape how you view the mission of God in your workplace? Is there something about how Jesus responds in this story that is pertinent to how you are being invited to respond to situations in your work?

Respond

The goal of this Bible study is not to create anxious activity but *prayerful response* to what God is revealing to you. Each week, there will be a practical way for you to respond to what you are learning that is directly related to your work.

Embodying beloved community

The invitation this week is to imagine what a beloved community could look like in your workplace. Kimberly Deckel says, "The fullness of the gospel calls us to four requests: the cultural mandate—go out and create flourishing; the great commission—go out and make disciples; the great commandment—love God and love others; and the great requirement—do justice and love mercy."[1] In many traditions, the great requirement is often an optional invitation from God, rather than a mandate that includes the industries and workplaces we inhabit. Yet justice and mercy are central to the very nature and action of God throughout the entire biblical story. The goal is not simply the absence of injustice but the creation of what Martin Luther King Jr. and others refer to as a

"beloved community." The vision and principles outlined by King may prove helpful in imagining such a community. For this response, we will explore the multifaceted nature of justice with the acronym GEAR (Generosity, Equality, Advocacy, and Responsibility), as well as some of the core aspects of creating a beloved community in our workplaces.

As a group, process these questions together:

- In your tradition and background, how central or peripheral have the concepts of mercy and justice been when it comes to viewing vocations and industries?

God's justice involves both retributive and reparative elements:

- **RETRIBUTIVE JUSTICE**: the dispensing of punishment for those who have caused harm and done wrong.

[1] Redeemer City to City, *The Missional Disciple: Pursuing Mercy and Justice at Work* (New York, NY: Redeemer City to City, 2022), Lesson 3 video.

- **REPARATIVE JUSTICE**: the restoration of those who are victims of injustice, which includes creating real belonging, repairing and reconciling relationships, and recognizing that victims of injustice not only need fair treatment but also have real contributions to make to the flourishing of a community.

- Can you share a story from your city, workplace, or community context where you have seen both forms of justice practiced? Which of the two do you think needs to be practiced more fully in your workplace?

- Which of the four aspects of biblical justice (Generosity, Equality, Advocacy, and Responsibility) do you most resonate with? Which one is hardest for you to grasp and practice? Below are some questions to consider in your workplace related to these four areas of biblical justice:

- **GENEROSITY**: As you go about your work this week, who in your company or industry regularly practices generosity toward others? If no one comes to mind, are there ways you can imagine this being expressed?

- **EQUALITY**: Are there areas in your workplace or industry where an individual or group are not being treated as image-bearers of God?

- **ADVOCACY**: Is there an issue in your workplace or industry where you could be advocating for the poor, weak, or powerless (or even a group that has less agency than you) in a way that reflects God's character?

- **RESPONSIBILITY**: With your current standing and power in your company or industry, where could you seek justice and repair in a way that enters into the suffering of others and works toward restoration?

Release

See the ending of each week together as a release into God's world for the good work he has called us to. Stand and recite this commissioning together each week:

God, you have made us in your image to care and cultivate your good creation.

However, we recognize our work is filled with thorns and thistles, injustice and mistreatment.

The world is not the way it is supposed to be.

Yet you have not abandoned your world, but through Jesus Christ you have sprouted forth seeds of new creation everywhere we look.

Holy Spirit, breath of the living God, send us now as partners with Christ into every industry to demonstrate and declare good news until Christ's return.

Notes

Week Five

Leader's Notes

Reflect

As you heard the story, what detail, phrase, or moment did the Holy Spirit use to grab your attention?

Trust that the Spirit of God is illuminating this story for your group and is ready to reveal insights and invitations for their participation in the mission of God.

Do you resonate more with Jairus or the woman in this story? Why?

The Gospel writer Mark intentionally contrasts these two characters in the story to showcase the kingdom of God to everyone, regardless of social status. Help people locate themselves in light of this.

As you watch Jesus respond to the situation unfolding, what insights do you glean about the mission of God?

After people identify themselves as the recipient of help from Jesus in the previous question, help them transition to reading this story from the perspective of Jesus as a model for our participation in mission.

How might this story shape how you view the mission of God in your workplace? Is there something about how Jesus responds in this story that is pertinent to how you are being invited to respond to situations in your work?

These questions help participants directly relate the mission of God to their work. Some of the insights you could point people toward could be:

- Who is ostracized from the community in your workplace that you could invite in?

- What interruptions in your work do you need to reimagine as opportunities for God to reveal himself, like in this story?

- What words of identity do people in your workplace need to hear, like Jesus' words to this woman?

- What are some of the ways hurriedness might prevent you from noticing what God is doing in your workplace?

Week Six

Work and Our Posture to the City

(1 PETER 2:9–12)

Introduction

Throughout history, God's people have been an oppressed minority. They have lived as exiles and have often been pressed to the margins of the world's largest empires. In all of this hostility, it would have been tempting for the people of God to live as a conclave isolated from the world. Yet from the Old to New Testament, the people of God have been invited to see their identity as both exiles and faithful citizens in the cities God has placed them. Jesus describes this identity as being "the salt of the earth" (Matthew 5:13). Salt can preserve that which is decomposing, but it can also accentuate the best of the flavors that already exist. This is our role in the city. We embrace the paradoxical identity of exiles and citizens. The passage today unpacks this vision from 1 Peter 2:9–12 and its intersection with our work.

Ready

The unbelievable truth is this: You are about to hear God speak. Every time you pick up the Bible, an encounter with God is possible. First, ready yourself to enter God's presence and hear his voice. To begin, offer this simple prayer to God and then wait in silence for two minutes:

Father, help me hear your voice.
Jesus, help me sense your presence.
Spirit, help me live according to your ways.

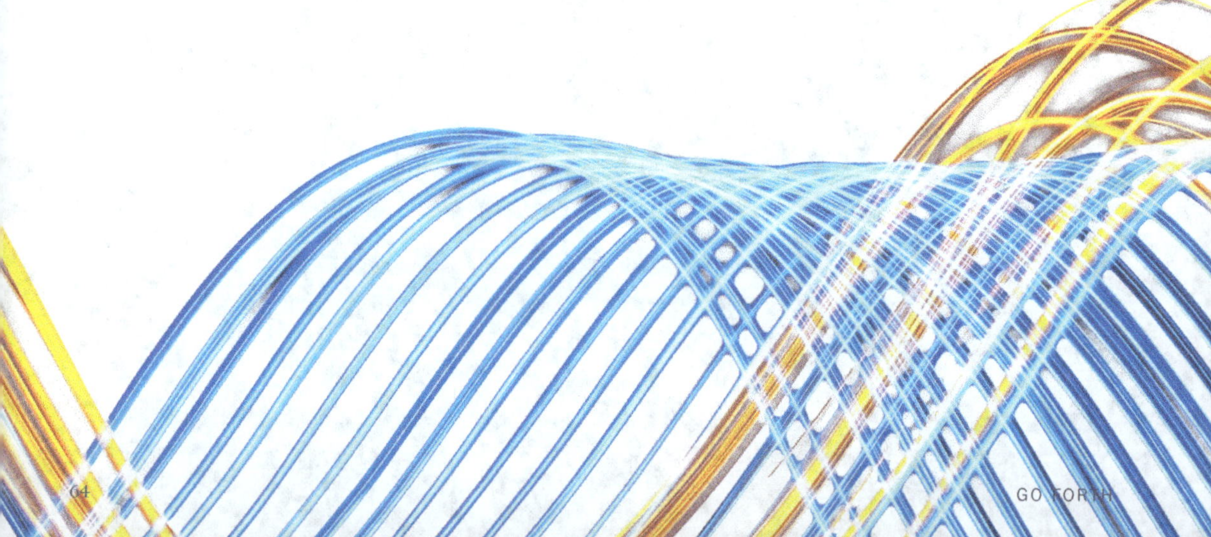

Read

After sitting in silence for two minutes, choose someone to read the passage below. Then choose a different person to read through the passage again.

1 Peter 2:9–12:

⁹ But you are a chosen race, **a royal priesthood, a holy nation, a people for his own possession**, that you may proclaim the excellencies of him who called you out of darkness into his marvelous light. ¹⁰ **Once you were not a people**, but now you are God's people; once you had not received mercy, but now you have received mercy.

¹¹ Beloved, I urge you as sojourners and exiles to abstain from the passions of the flesh, which wage war against your soul. ¹² Keep your conduct among the Gentiles honorable, so that when they speak against you as evildoers, **they may see your good deeds and glorify God** on the day of visitation.

Key References

"A royal priesthood, a holy nation, a people for his own possession" (2:9): Do these identity markers sound familiar? They are the same words used to describe the Israelites in Exodus 19:5–6 as they ventured into a new land. What Peter says here is that Christians carry this same identity: a people set apart by God, at least in part for the sake of their neighbors encountering what God is like through their shared lives.

"Once you were not a people" (2:10): This entire verse is a quotation from Hosea 2:23: "And I will have mercy on No Mercy, and I will say to Not My People, 'You are my people'; and he shall say, 'You are my God.'" God is clarifying the identity of the Christians addressed in 1 Peter who were scattered throughout the Roman Empire and may feel overlooked or oppressed in light of their status as Christians.

"They may see your good deeds and glorify God" (2:12): In English Bibles, there is typically a paragraph change after 1 Peter 2:10. But what if we read verses 11–12 as an outworking of the identity markers of 2:9–10? In other words, the people of God have been chosen to live a different way of life not for the sake of separating themselves from the city, but so that their watching neighbors might catch a glimpse of God and glorify him.

Reflect

The aim of this section is for you to dialogue as a group about what insights and questions come to mind as you hear God's Word. Use the discussion questions below to guide the conversation.

- Which moment, phrase, or detail of the passage is the Holy Spirit grabbing your attention with?

- Which of the identity markers in 1 Peter 2:9–10 resonate most with you right now?

- In your part of the city, what "passions" of the flesh are most alluring?

- As you understand your role as God's priestly people, what good deeds do you currently display to your neighbors? What about in your workplace?

- Ten years from now, what fruit do you hope to see in the industry and workplace you inhabit by your faithful presence there? What stories would you like to tell?

Respond

The goal of this Bible study is not to create anxious activity but *prayerful response* to what God is revealing to you. Each week, there will be a practical way for you to respond to what you are learning that is directly related to your work.

The creation-fall-redemption lens

The invitation this week is to re-narrate the story of your work to a coworker or colleague. This will involve articulating a Creation-Fall-Redemption lens for someone in your industry or workplace. Let's reframe how Jesus might view the best version of peoples' industries. As an example, you can look at the work of janitors and custodians through the Creation-Fall-Redemption framework below.

How might your work fit into this framework?

INDUSTRY: CLEANING SERVICES (JANITORS/CUSTODIANS)		
CREATION	**FALL**	**REDEMPTION**
Humanity's mandate from Genesis 1 was to steward God's good creation so that all might flourish. The role of the janitor or custodian is to steward a space for others to use and flourish in. They do this by mopping floors, tending to trash, refilling toilet paper in bathrooms, solving problems, or fixing things that are broken.	The creation God made has been marred by sin, sickness, and disease. Within this industry, janitors are often given the task of responding to the consequences of sin: destroyed property, spills and stains, overflowing toilets, pests, and building damages. As employees, they are often overlooked, working invisible hours to maintain an environment with little to no recognition.	Jesus was the Great Janitor/Custodian who took on the sicknesses and diseases of the world, cleansing hearts, bodies, and spaces. Janitors/custodians do the hidden work of disinfecting spaces, preventing the spread of millions of germs and diseases. They keep walkways and floors clear of debris and spills so that others might flourish as they walk through them.

Release

See the ending of each week together as a release into God's world for the good work he has called us to. Stand and recite this commissioning together each week:

God, you have made us in your image to care and cultivate your good creation.

However, we recognize our work is filled with thorns and thistles, injustice and mistreatment.

The world is not the way it is supposed to be.

Yet you have not abandoned your world, but through Jesus Christ you have sprouted forth seeds of new creation everywhere we look.

Holy Spirit, breath of the living God, send us now as partners with Christ into every industry to demonstrate and declare good news until Christ's return.

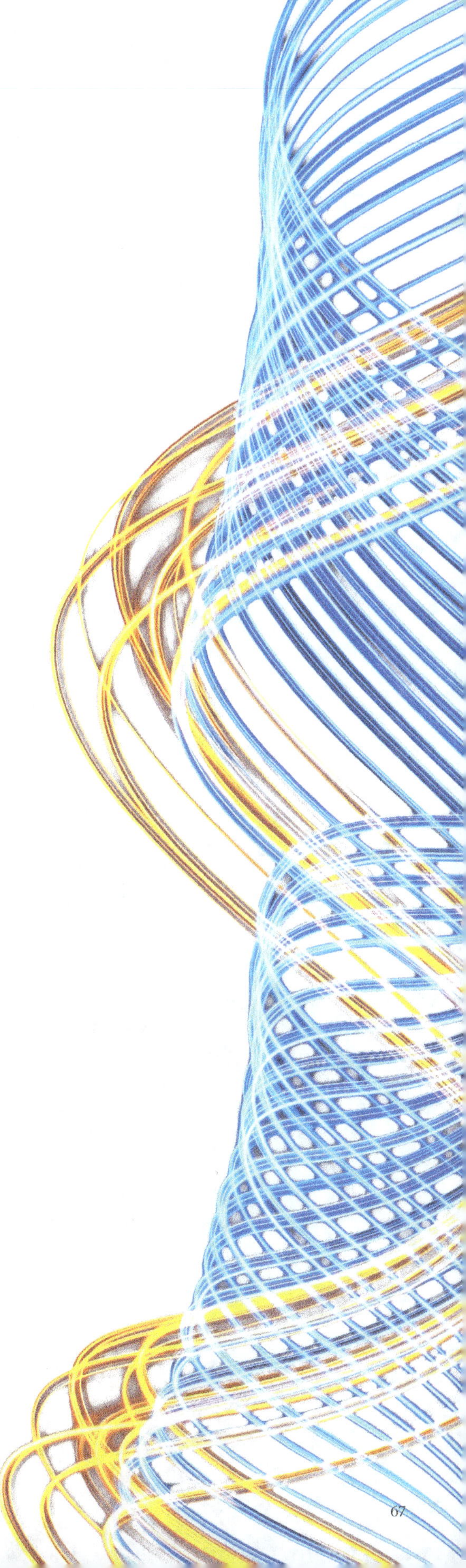

Notes

Week Six

Leader's Notes

Reflect

Which moment, phrase, or detail of the passage is the Holy Spirit grabbing your attention with?

Every time we open Scripture, God is seeking to get our attention. You might be surprised at how your participants answer this question, and it will allow the group to speak good news to one another as you listen together.

Which of the identity markers in 1 Peter 2:9–10 resonate most with you right now?

Some of the identity markers participants could say are: chosen people, royal priesthood, holy nation, people for God's possession, those who received mercy. Whatever identity markers individuals in your group choose, have them work to explain why this identity comforts, convicts, or challenges them in a fresh way.

In your part of the city, what "passions" of the flesh are most alluring?

When Paul is referring to "passions" here, he could have a number of different realities in mind. Often "passions" can be the good things of creation that get twisted and become idolatrous. Another way to phrase this question would be: What are people chasing in pursuit of the "good life" in your city?

As you understand your role as God's priestly people, what good deeds do you currently display to your neighbors? What about in your workplace?

Have your group work hard to give tangible yet simple ways they put God on display.

Ten years from now, what fruit do you hope to see in the industry and workplace you inhabit by your faithful presence there? What stories would you like to tell?

This is an imagination exercise. The goal is to dream together in the midst of work often being a place of drudgery and survival. You are imagining together how the world should be and will be one day.

Week Seven

Justice and
Work

(LUKE 3:1–18)

Introduction

This week, we are entering into a contested space: how mercy and justice intersect with your work. Across your city, there are competing visions of justice, and many Christians are confused about what biblical justice should look like. For some Christians, justice might seem like an optional extra that is unessential to our witness. Yet mercy and justice were and still are central to the ministry of Jesus, as he is on a mission to reconcile all people and all things to himself and bring permanent peace to creation (Colossians 1:19–20). How might our daily work be an avenue to embody the mercy and justice of God? How might we have opportunities to take up our role as ambassadors of reconciliation (2 Corinthians 5:16–20)?

The cities we inhabit long for a more compelling, holistic, and rooted vision of justice and mercy. Our faithful presence in workplaces and industries can give a glimpse and taste of the kingdom on earth as it is in heaven.

Ready

The unbelievable truth is this: You are about to hear God speak. Every time you pick up the Bible, an encounter with God is possible. First, ready yourself to enter God's presence and hear his voice. To begin, offer this simple prayer to God and then wait in silence for two minutes:

Father, help me hear your voice.
Jesus, help me sense your presence.
Spirit, help me live according to your ways.

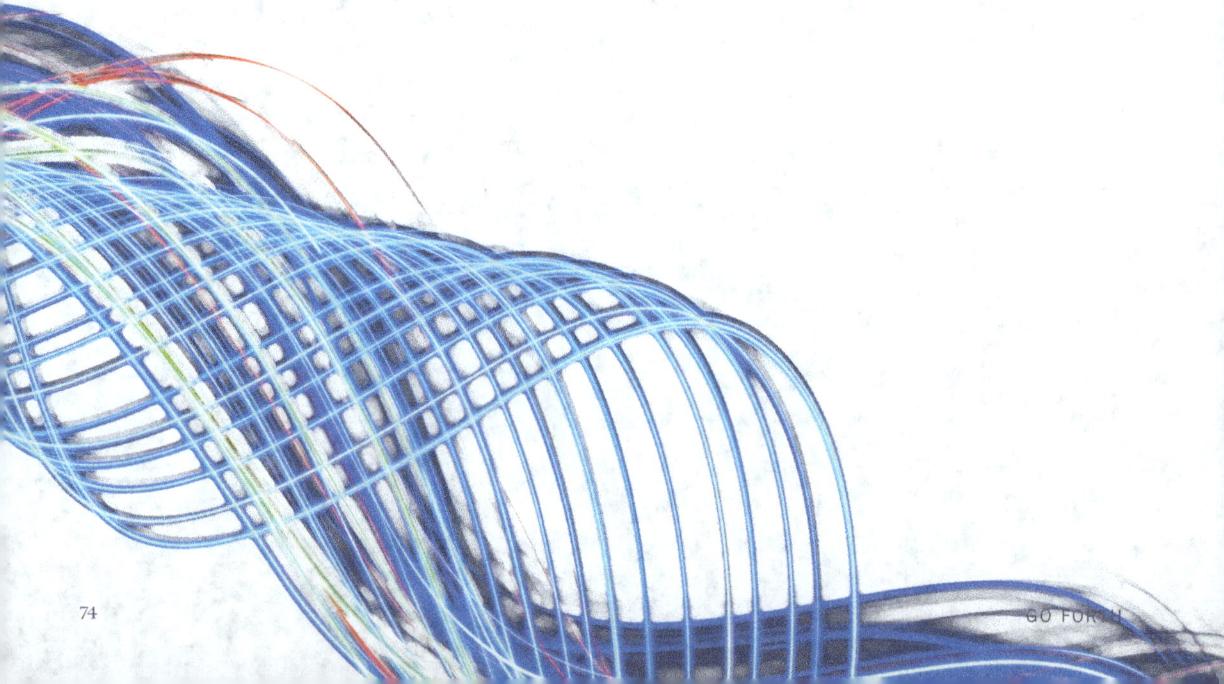

Read

After sitting in silence for two minutes, choose someone to read the passage below. Then choose a different person to read through the passage again.

Luke 3:1-18:

[1] In the fifteenth year of the reign of Tiberius Caesar, Pontius Pilate being governor of Judea, and Herod being tetrarch of Galilee, and his brother Philip tetrarch of the region of Ituraea and Trachonitis, and Lysanias tetrarch of Abilene, [2] during the high priesthood of Annas and Caiaphas, the word of God came to John the son of Zechariah in the wilderness. [3] And he went into all the region **around the Jordan**, proclaiming a baptism of repentance for the forgiveness of sins. [4] As it is written in the book of the words of Isaiah the prophet,

> "The voice of one crying in the wilderness: 'Prepare the way of the Lord, make his paths straight.
> [5] Every valley shall be filled, and every mountain and hill shall be made low, and the crooked shall become straight, and the rough places shall become level ways,
> [6] and all flesh shall see the salvation of God.'"

[7] He said therefore to the crowds that came out to be baptized by him, "You brood of vipers! Who warned you to flee from the wrath to come? [8] Bear fruits in keeping with repentance. And do not begin to say to yourselves, 'We have Abraham as our father.' For I tell you, God is able from these stones to raise up children for Abraham. [9] Even now the axe is laid to the root of the trees. Every tree therefore that does not bear good fruit is cut down and thrown into the fire."

[10] And the crowds asked him, "**What then shall we do?**" [11] And he answered them, "Whoever has two tunics is to share with him who has none, and whoever has food is to do likewise." [12] Tax collectors also came to be baptized and said to him, "Teacher, what shall we do?" [13] And he said to them, "Collect no more than you are authorized to do." [14] Soldiers also asked him, "And we, what shall we do?" And he said to them, "Do not extort money from anyone by threats or by false accusation, and be content with your wages."

[15] As the people were in expectation, and all were questioning in their hearts concerning John, whether he might be the Christ, [16] John answered them all, saying, "I baptize you with water, but he who is mightier than I is coming, the strap of whose sandals I am not worthy to untie. He will baptize you with the Holy Spirit and fire. [17] His winnowing fork is in his hand, to clear his threshing floor and to gather the wheat into his barn, but the chaff he will burn with unquenchable fire." [18] So with many other exhortations he preached good news to the people.

Key References

"Around the Jordan" (3:3): This small detail can be easy to miss, but it is important. Centuries before, the people of God crossed the Jordan River to enter into the Promised Land (Joshua 3). As John is calling people to be baptized in the Jordan River, he is inviting them to ready themselves for a new exodus journey, to a new promised land that is inaugurated in the coming of the Messiah, King Jesus.

"What then shall we do?" (3:10): This is a valid question for people who recognize their need for repentance. In response, John gives them a concrete action plan related to their resources and daily work! If you have two pairs of clothes (tunics) or extra food, give some away to someone in need (3:11). If your job is a tax collector, don't exploit those you are collecting from for personal gain (3:12 –13). If you are serving in the military, don't make accusations of civilians and be content with your pay (3:14). In other words, John sees the entry point to readying yourself for the coming kingdom of God as engaging in mercy and justice.

Reflect

The aim of this section is for you to dialogue as a group about what insights and questions come to mind as you hear God's Word. Use the discussion questions below to guide the conversation.

- As you heard the story, what moment, phrase, or detail was the Holy Spirit using to grab your attention?

- In your own words, how would you describe John's message to the crowds? How does it sit with you?

- In the passage, John gives specific instructions to two ancient types of work: tax collectors and soldiers. If John were to address your vocation, what areas of mercy or justice would he potentially challenge you about?

Respond

The goal of this Bible study is not to create anxious activity but *prayerful response* to what God is revealing to you. Each week, there will be a practical way for you to respond to what you are learning that is directly related to your work.

Becoming a restorative presence

The invitation this week is to explore the idea of becoming a restorative presence in your workplace.

Being a restorative presence in your work includes three primary practices:

1. Being rooted in Christ

2. Being cultivators of community

3. Being advocates of justice in systems and structures

- In your current workplace, in which of these three do you feel strongest? In which do you feel weakest?

- Can you think of a destructive presence in your workplace? What is the result?

- Of the three practices outlined above to become a restorative presence, which one could you tangibly practice this week?

Some examples could be:

- "I want to practice being rooted in Christ by praying on the way to and from work for the kindness of God to radiate through me toward coworkers, clients, and even those who are difficult for me to love."

- "I want to practice inviting an overlooked member of my work team to lunch to get to know them and hear more of their story as I seek to be a cultivator of community."

- "I want to practice advocating against an unjust practice in my workplace (e.g., pay inequality, production shortcuts, or deceptive marketing) by both seeking to acknowledge why I believe it is broken and offering an alternative solution."

Release

See the ending of each week together as a release into God's world for the good work he has called us to. Stand and recite this commissioning together each week:

God, you have made us in your image to care and cultivate your good creation.

However, we recognize our work is filled with thorns and thistles, injustice and mistreatment.

The world is not the way it is supposed to be.

Yet you have not abandoned your world, but through Jesus Christ you have sprouted forth seeds of new creation everywhere we look.

Holy Spirit, breath of the living God, send us now as partners with Christ into every industry to demonstrate and declare good news until Christ's return.

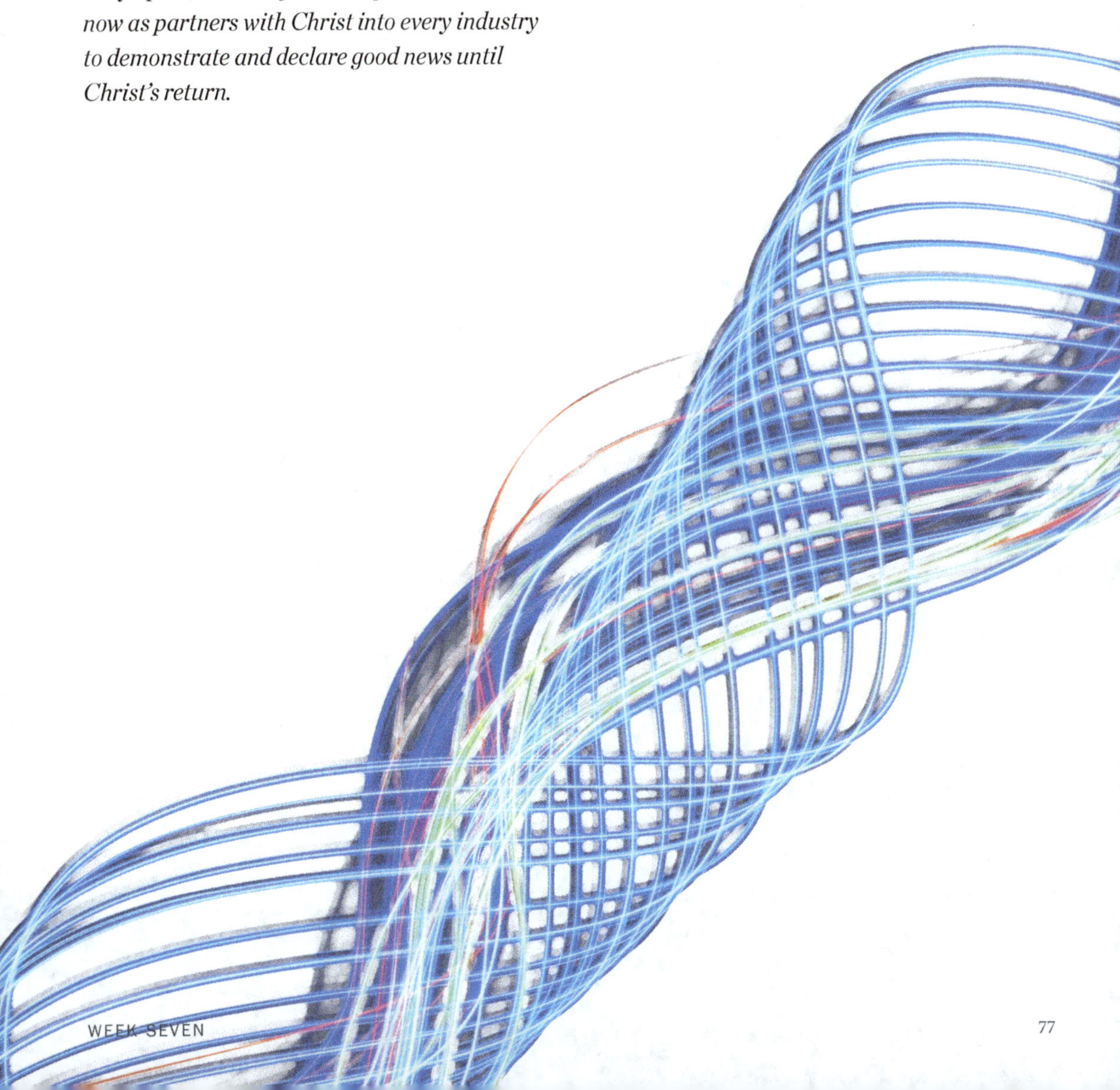

Notes

Week
Seven

Leader's
Notes

Reflect

As you heard the story, what moment, phrase, or detail was the Holy Spirit using to grab your attention?

This is an open-ended question to create dialogue and potential directions for the conversation.

In your own words, how would you describe John's message to the crowds? How does it sit with you?

The goal of this question is to help people synthesize the message of John. But the hope is that participants recognize how central mercy and justice are to the coming of the kingdom of God.

In the passage, John gives specific instructions to two ancient types of work: tax collectors and soldiers. If John were to address your vocation, what areas of mercy or justice would he potentially challenge you about?

Have people think long and hard about what John might say to their industry or workplace. What would he demand as the "fruit of repentance" (Luke 3:8)? The goal is for people to begin imagining mercy and justice as integral aspects of their work.

Week Eight

Work and the
Future Kingdom

Introduction

Many Christians imagine eternity with God as a never-ending vacation of leisure and relaxation. And although there will be incredible rest and delight in God's presence, there will also be good work to do. But this will be work unlike anything we have experienced on earth; it is work untarnished by the thorns and thistles of sin's curse. It will be totally satisfying and meaningful, and even the jobs we most overlook on earth will be rightfully celebrated. We will experience the perfect rhythm of work and rest alongside our Creator. We get a taste of this vision in the book of Revelation where the radiance of God will fill the streets of the New Jerusalem, and humans will reign alongside God (Revelation 5:10; Revelation 21–22).

This future new Creation will bring together the best of our paid and unpaid work. But, because of Jesus' death and resurrection, that future has also been brought into the present. Instead of waiting for full redemption to finally be accomplished, we can participate now in the glimpses and echoes of restorative work. Thanks to Christ, we can taste a little of what the New Jerusalem will be like in our everyday work.

Ready

The unbelievable truth is this: You are about to hear God speak. Every time you pick up the Bible, an encounter with God is possible. First, ready yourself to enter God's presence and hear his voice. To begin, offer this simple prayer to God and then wait in silence for two minutes:

Father, help me hear your voice.
Jesus, help me sense your presence.
Spirit, help me live according to your ways.

Read

After sitting in silence for two minutes, choose someone to read the passage below. Then choose a different person to read through the passage again.

Revelation 22:1–7:

[1] Then the angel showed me the river of the water of life, bright as crystal, flowing from the throne of God and of the Lamb [2] through the middle of the street of the **city**; also, on either side of the river, the tree of life with its twelve kinds of fruit, yielding its fruit each month. The leaves of the tree were for the healing of the nations. [3] No longer will there be anything accursed, but the throne of God and of the Lamb will be in it, and his servants will worship him. [4] They will see his face, and his name will be on their foreheads. [5] And night will be no more. They will need no light of lamp or sun, for the Lord God will be their light, and they will reign forever and ever.

[6] And he said to me, "These words are trustworthy and true. And the Lord, the God of the spirits of the prophets, has sent his angel to show his servants what must soon take place."

[7] "And behold, I am coming soon. Blessed is the one who keeps the words of the prophecy of this book."

Key References

"City" (22:2): For many Christians, they imagine new creation as a "return" to the garden of Eden and the primitive beginning of Adam and Eve. However, God's desire was not for the garden to remain a garden forever. Through the work and cultivation of humans, the garden would be transformed into a Garden City— hence the language in this passage, and Revelation 21 is a mixture of both garden and city.

Reflect

The aim of this section is for you to dialogue about what insights and questions come to mind as you hear God's Word. Use the discussion questions below to guide the conversation.

- As you heard the passage, what words, phrases, or moments grabbed your attention? What brings you hope and encouragement?

- The passage describes a city with a river running through it (vv. 1–2). How does the end of the story here differ from the beginning of the story in Genesis 1–2?

- The passage says, "They will reign forever and ever" (v. 5). What do you think that means for us?

- Are there ways you can imagine your work contributing to the eventual Holy City that will exist in the New Heavens and the New Earth?

Respond

The goal of this Bible study is not to create anxious activity but *prayerful response* to what God is revealing to you. Each week, there will be a practical way for you to respond to what you are learning that is directly related to your work.

Headlines of new creation

This week, you are invited to an imagination exercise called "Headlines of New Creation." This exercise is to help you see what your work and industry might be like in restored creation. Each person will craft a headline of a story that could be told about their industry and workplace in light of everything being restored and made new in Jesus. This might feel like a challenging assignment, but lean on your group to help imagine together.

- What would the headline read?

- What stories would be told in the small print in light of this headline?

- What is happening in your industry in renewed creation?

Release

See the ending of each week together as a
release into God's world for the good work
he has called us to. Stand and recite this
commissioning together each week:

*God, you have made us in your image to care
and cultivate your good creation.*

*However, we recognize our work is filled with
thorns and thistles, injustice and mistreatment.*

The world is not the way it is supposed to be.

*Yet you have not abandoned your world, but
through Jesus Christ you have sprouted forth
seeds of new creation everywhere we look.*

*Holy Spirit, breath of the living God, send us
now as partners with Christ into every industry
to demonstrate and declare good news until
Christ's return.*

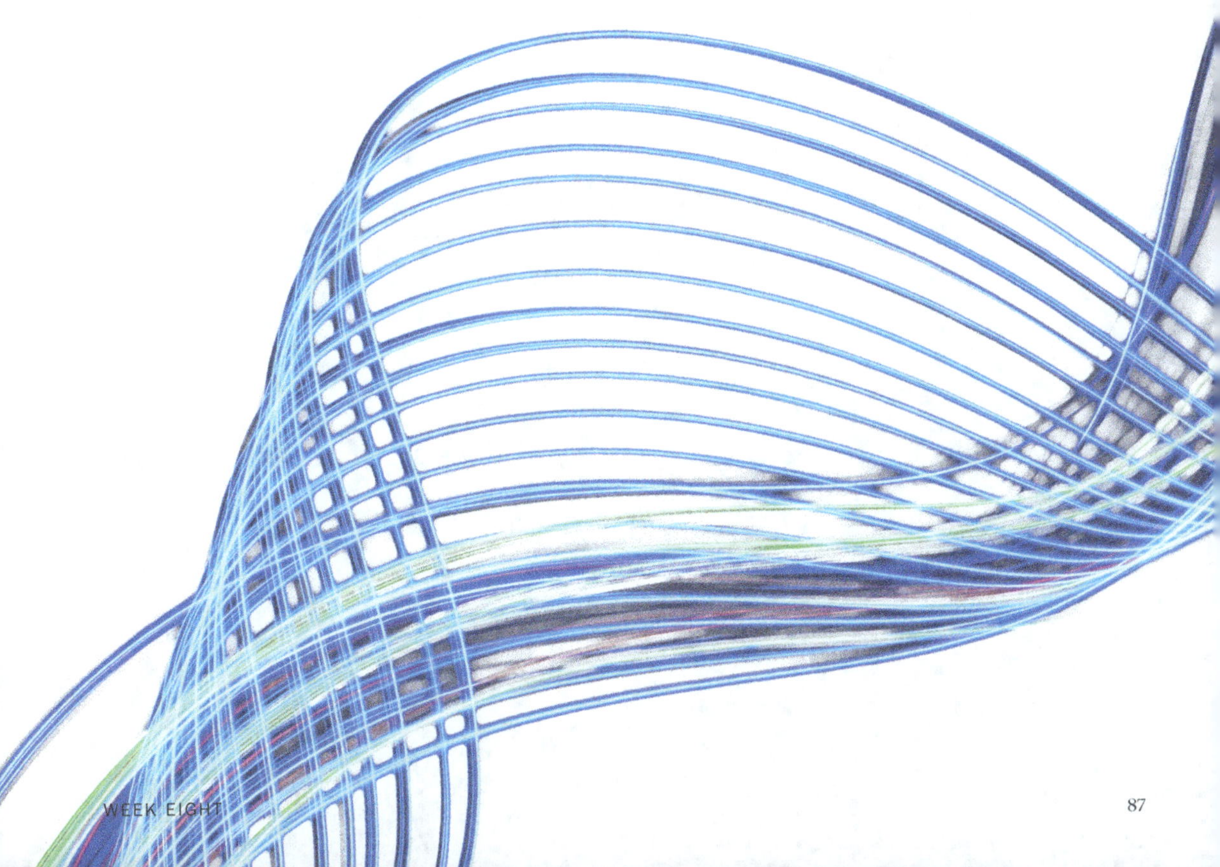

Notes

Week Eight

Leader's
Notes

Reflect

As you heard the passage, what words, phrases, or moments grabbed your attention? What brings you hope and encouragement?

The goal of this question is to create an open dialogue where the Holy Spirit can begin speaking and illuminating the text to your particular group.

The passage describes a city with a river running through it (vv. 1–2). How does the end of the story here differ from the beginning of the story in Genesis 1–2?

There is an intentional overlap in the language of Revelation 21–22 with Genesis 1–2, but there is a key difference: The picture of the garden has been transformed to include a city. The goal of this question is to help people imagine the new Creation not as a return to a garden but as an indwelling of God with his people in a Garden City.

The passage says, "They will reign forever and ever" (v. 5). What do you think that means for us?

The goal of this question is for people to recognize the new Creation not as a place of leisure-like passivity but as participation in meaningful and good work, reigning alongside Jesus the King. Again, the goal is for people to imagine what this might look like.

Are there ways you can imagine your work contributing to the eventual Holy City that will exist in the New Heavens and the New Earth?

The fundamental reality in God's story is that our work is not just temporary but has eternal implications. Something about the work we are participating in now will carry over into the work involved in the New Jerusalem. To help respond to this question, you could choose one participant to share about their work/industry. Then, as a group, brainstorm what their current work could look like in the Holy City.

Example: an accountant. In the Holy City, there will be projects that will need the work of skilled accountants to properly organize the funding, resources, and numbers related to the work. Accountants help make sense of all the math and numbers involved in every task. Accountants make sure no resources are wasted or abused but rather everything is stewarded for the flourishing of all.

Contributors

Lauren Gill
General Editor

Lauren is the senior director of the Global Faith & Work Initiative at Redeemer City to City, where she works with pastors, church planters and ministry leaders around the world to equip their lay leaders to push against brokenness in every industry and field. She is a coauthor and the general editor of *The Missional Disciple: Pursuing Mercy & Justice at Work* and a coauthor of a forthcoming book on how to build a faith and work ministry. Prior to working for City to City, she worked at the Center for Faith & Work at Redeemer Presbyterian Church in New York City. She is a licensed mental health counselor in New York State and has counseled individuals on vocational issues. She holds an MA in Counseling Psychology from Columbia University and a BFA from New York University in Drama and Journalism. She lives in New York City with her husband, Suneel, and their two children.

Charlie Meo
Author

Charlie is passionate about making meaningful resources for disciples of Jesus. He currently serves as the curriculum director for the Surge Network and has been a regular contributor with Redeemer City to City. He has experience serving as a pastor in a missional church movement and also teaching in the classroom. He received a bachelor's degree from Biola University and a master's degree in Missional Theology from The Missional Training Center. Charlie and his wife, Keaton, are raising three children in Tempe, Arizona.

Redeemer City to City (CTC) is a non-profit organization that prayerfully recruits, trains, coaches and resources leaders who cultivate gospel movements in global cities primarily through church planting. CTC is based in New York City and works in over 75 global cities throughout Africa, Asia, Australia, North America, Latin America, the Middle East and Europe. CTC's core competencies are urban church planting, leadership development and content creation. All of this is done to help bring the gospel of Jesus Christ to cities.

For more information about Redeemer City to City, please visit **redeemercitytocity.com**.

The Global Faith & Work Initiative (GFWI) is a ministry of Redeemer City to City. GFWI equips, connects and mobilizes churches and city networks around the world for gospel-centered faith and work ministry with consulting, resources and training.

If you enjoyed the material in *Go Forth*, please visit **globalfaithandwork.com** for more resources to integrate your faith and work and to sign up for our newsletter.

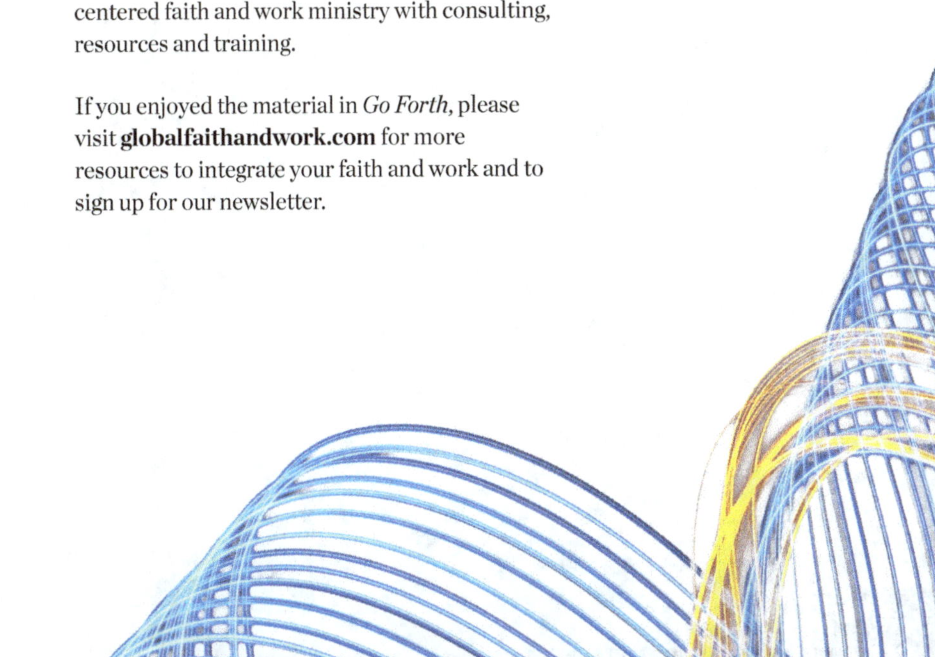

www.ingramcontent.com/pod-product-compliance
Lightning Source LLC
Chambersburg PA
CBHW081916120726
47996CB00010B/3351